Law and Behavioral Sciences

Law and Behavioral Sciences

Why We Need Less Purity Rather Than More

A shorter version of this text was presented as inaugural speech, held on the occasion of accepting the chair of Empirical Legal Studies at the Erasmus University Rotterdam on March 11, 2016

by

Peter Mascini

eleven
international publishing

Published, sold and distributed by Eleven International Publishing
P.O. Box 85576
2508 CG The Hague
The Netherlands
Tel.: +31 70 33 070 33
Fax: +31 70 33 070 30
e-mail: sales@elevenpub.nl
www.elevenpub.com

Sold and distributed in USA and Canada
International Specialized Book Services
920 NE 58th Avenue, Suite 300
Portland, OR 97213-3786, USA
Tel: 1-800-944-6190 (toll-free)
Fax: +1-503-280-8832
orders@isbs.com
www.isbs.com

Eleven International Publishing is an imprint of Boom uitgevers Den Haag.

ISBN 978-94-6236-679-4
ISBN 978-94-6274-551-3 (E-book)

Printed in The Netherlands

Introduction

In 2013, Michael Faure and Willem Van Boom asked me to join their ranks in managing the research program entitled *Behavioral Approaches to Contract and Tort* (BACT). It did not take me long to accept this honorable invitation. It also didn't take me long to realize that I had ended up in an academic environment, which was rather alien to me. I was the only sociologist in BACT. The other members of the research program study law from a legal, economical, or psychological perspective.

I want to use my inaugural speech to reflect upon my position as a sociologist in the behavioral study of law. I do this by positioning myself in relation to no less than three such approaches: law and economics, behavioral economics, and behavioral sociology. During the last few decades, law and economics and behavioral economics have boomed. It is mainly economists and psychologists who have contributed to these massive branches of research. However, in sociology there exists an older tradition in the behavioral study of law. This rather isolated, albeit influential school of thought is primarily based on the work of Donald Black and his successors. Hence, I will reflect upon a small body of sociological literature and two huge movements dominated by economists and psychologists.

Although few direct links exist between behavioral sociology and law and economics, they share a desire for purity in the behavioral study of law. With scientific purity I mean the deliberate choice to postulate a limited number of universally applicable behavioral principles. The guiding principle of behavioral sociology is that law behaves in correspondence to social space, while the guiding principle of mainstream law and economics is that individuals behave rationally. Behavioral economists have challenged this principle of the rational actor and, consequently, have also challenged the desire for scientific purity in law and economics. My own goal is to defend a two-fold thesis: first, that the purification of sociology proposed by behavioral sociology is a blind alley that can only be exited by allowing impurity. And second, that the behavioral economics movement has offered mainstream law and economics an opportunity to reinvigorate by embracing impurity. The combination of the two parts of my thesis lead me to the claim that we need less purity in the behavioral study of law rather than more. I will end my lecture by stating that the introduction of impurity that has been started by behavioral economics needs to be persisted in several respects.

I will address the first part of my thesis by briefly summarizing the essence of what behavioral sociology entails. Subsequently, I will describe its pure epistemology and the criticism it has ensued. I will end the first part of my thesis by arguing that several of these criticisms can be countered by allowing impurity. I will start addressing the second part of my thesis by first explaining what is mainstream law and economics. Subsequently, I will describe how behavioral economics has challenged the main assumption underlying law and economics and how the latter has responded to this challenge. I will end my lecture by clarifying what I mean when I say that the behavioral study of law needs less purity rather than more.

Black's behavioral sociology

Donald Black's (1976) concise book *The Behavior of Law* forms the base of behavioral sociology. Black conceives of law as a specific form of social control; social control by the state. He defines social control as the definition of and reaction to deviant behavior. He is completely agnostic as to what is designated deviant and normal behavior. Drinking cow's milk may be a sin in one context and completely normal in another. Black's conception of law differs fundamentally from that of legal scholars. While lawyers conceive law as a normative system, Black understands law as a form of quantifiable behavior that can be objectively established. The quantity of law increases, for example, with a call to the police, an arrest, a lawsuit, a victory for the prosecution or plaintiff, and the severity of a remedy (Black, D. 1995: 832).

Black's framework predicts how variation in legal life is related to its location and direction in social space. Black distinguishes five dimensions in social space: the vertical, the horizontal, the cultural, the collective, and the normative.[1] Based on these five dimensions of social space, behavioral sociology predicts how law behaves.

1 The vertical dimension or stratification concerns the allocation of scarce means in societies. The horizontal or morphological dimension consists of the dimensions task differentiation, relational distance – the extent to which people participate in each other's lives – and integration – or the extent to which people belong to the center or the margin of social life. The cultural or symbolic dimension consists of the dimensions density of ideas, conventionality of lifestyles, and cultural distance between groups in society. The organizational or collective dimension concerns the extent to which collective action takes place. The social control dimension, finally, consists of the dimension concerning the definition of and reaction to deviant behavior by other means than the law and the dimension of respectability.

Some of these predictions concern linear connections – for example, regarding the vertical dimension Black predicts: "law varies directly with stratification" and "downward law is greater than upward law." Other predictions are curvilinear. For instance, concerning the cultural dimension Black predicts: "law is less likely at the extremes, where there is little or no cultural diversity, and also where it is great." He also predicts how law evolves (Black, D. 1976: 132-7). The transition from primitive to modern society is accompanied by a concomitant transition from anarchy to law. This transition is due to the expansion of social space: stratification, relational distance, culture and collective behavior increase, while informal social control decreases. How law will behave in response to the transition from modern to postmodern society is uncertain because the extremes of different social dimensions get increasingly entangled. For instance, globalization enables intimate relationships between utter strangers, imploding the horizontal dimension. As a result of these contradictory social developments, law will probably change fundamentally and may eventually even disappear altogether.

Behavioral sociologists are convinced that the geometrical theory of law is universally applicable, and I quote: "Legal codes vary across jurisdictions, changing with the passage of time and geographical distance. The sociological laws that determine the use of discretion [in applying the law], however, are general and unchanging" (Baumgartner, M. P. 1984). Following the success of the volume *The Behavior of Law*, behavioral sociologists have aimed at developing a general theory of social behavior. First, by including other actors that are involved in legal conflicts besides litigants. Allegedly, the more is known about the location in social space of the whole social configuration involved in a legal conflict, the better the behavior of law can be predicted. For example, taking into account how the coordinates of legal officials compare to those of the conflicting parties explains why judges treat police officers suspected of committing a crime more leniently than they do civilians (Baumgartner, M. P. 1984, Black, D. 1993). After all, the social distance between judges and police officers is smaller than it is between judges and civilians.

A second move towards generating a general theory of social behavior consists of applying the framework to other social phenomena besides law. First to informal social control, or what Black designates as *self-help* – "the expression of a grievance by unilateral aggression" (Black, D. 1983). For example, after the attacks of 9/11, Black (2004) has applied his framework to terrorism.[2] Black explains terrorism by social geometry – its multidimensional location and direction in social space. Terrorism arises inter-collectively and upwardly across long relational distances. Allegedly, this renders terrorism a modern phenomenon: "because social distance historically corresponded to physical distance, terrorism often lacked the physical geometry necessary for its occurrence: physical closeness to civilians socially distant enough to attract terrorism. New technology has made physical distance between socially distant groups increasingly irrelevant, hence terrorism has proliferated" Black (2004: 20/1). Subsequently, Black (1993) has integrated his work on law and self-help into an overarching theory of social control in *The Social Structure of Right and Wrong*. Later on he has also applied his framework on other social phenomenon such as art and science (Black, D. 2013). Finally, he has expanded his framework in order to predict social change by introducing the concept of social time as the dynamic dimension of social space (Black, D. 2011).

THE EPISTEMOLOGY OF BEHAVIORAL SOCIOLOGY

Behavioral sociologists' ambitions to come up with a universal theory of social behavior are based on a positivist epistemology.[3] Black (1995, 2000a/b) has set out his epistemology in publications with telling titles such as '*The Purification of Sociology*', '*The Epistemology of Pure Sociology*', and '*Dreams of Pure Sociology*'. Black aspires value-free science. In his opinion, modern sociology is devoid of value-free science because it is still classical. Like classical sociologists, modern sociologists still nearly always explain human behavior *teleologically* – as a means to an end, *psychologically* – as something that arises at least partially in the human mind, and *individualistically* – as the behavior of people. Since Black deems

2 Terrorism is defined as self-help by organized civilians who covertly inflict mass violence on other civilians' (Black, D. 2004: 14).

3 Ryan (2015) is right arguing there is no agreed upon definition of positivism. He argues that the list of indicators of positivism is incoherent and that some indicators conflict, and he proposes to focus on these more concrete indicators rather than treating positivism as an encompassing paradigm. However, since behavioral sociology scores high on many of these indicators and low on none of them, I deem it defendable to qualify behavioral sociology as a positivist paradigm.

modern sociology unscientific and not social, he proposes to revolutionize sociology.

Revolutionary sociology addresses social life and nothing else. Social life has its own ontology – a distinctive existence entirely unlike any person or a person's thoughts. "Although everyone is an agent of social life, social life itself is drastically different from any person. It has no mind. It has no subjectivity. It is observable and explainable without regard to the thoughts and feelings of the individual involved" (Black, D. 2000: 706). Examples, are law, violence, art, and science, including sociology itself. Black continues by stating: "My paradigm removes people from the center of the social universe. It deprives people of their explanatory importance" (Black, D. 1995: 866). It also sticks to observable phenomena, and only those phenomena. [After all,] assumptions or assertions about anything in the human mind introduce a fog of uncertainty into any formulation (Black, D. 1995: 850). Hence, empirically meaningless value statements are eliminated from my paradigm.[4]

How successful has been the attempt to come up with a universal theory of social behavior based on a positivist epistemology?

Praise and disapproval

Black has distinguished five criteria determining the quality of a theory – testability, generality, simplicity, validity, and originality (Black, D. 1995). He has applied these criteria to his own work and concludes, maybe not entirely surprisingly, that it scores high on all five criteria. Therefore, he asserts that "no comparably general theory of law has been attempted... and no theory is presently imaginable... and in its ability to make unexpected discoveries, is on par with the theories of Hubble and Einstein" (Black, D. 1995: 834; Marshall, D. A. 2008: 216). This quote may suggest we are dealing with a pathologically overconfident scholar. However, Black is certainly not alone in praising his work. For example, as the blurb on the back cover shows, *The Behavior of Law* was immediately welcomed a classic and designated the most important contribution

---

4 While classical sociologists measure solidarity based on the extent to which people feel connected to others, Senechal de la Roche (2001) measures solidarity 'objectively' based on the extent to which people participate in each other's lives, differentiate tasks, and share the same lifestyle. Black measures respectability, for example, based on the clothes people wear, whether or not they have a criminal record or distinctions rather than their esteem in the eyes of others.

ever made to the sociology of law and more. Black's stature has been compared with that of Emile Durkheim, one of the three founding fathers of sociology and he has received many awards. He also has many followers and admirers (for example, Baumgartner, Collins, Cooney, Horwitz, Senechal-de la Roche).

However, behavioral sociology has also elicited fierce criticism. One category of criticism boils down to the argument that behavioral sociology is antithetical to the very scientific values that Black invokes to justify it. This category of criticisms can, in principle, be solved within the remit of Black's epistemology. Another category of criticisms imply that the shortcomings of behavioral sociology emanate directly from its aim to purify sociology. This category of criticisms are of a more fundamental nature because they argue that the problems originate from within the epistemology itself. These problems can only be solved by abandoning the positivist epistemology. I will briefly summarize both types of criticism.

Sinning against one's own principles

Why is it argued that behavioral sociology is antithetical to the very same scientific values it propagates?

First, an approach that aims to achieve objectivity may be expected to define and measure theoretical concepts clearly. However, this goal is not delivered.[5] This lack of conceptual clarity concerns, among others, the five dimensions of social space. Although Black designates social space a theoretical concept, it can merely be conceived of a metaphor (Hunt, A. 1983: 29-31).[6] "Black associates stratification with the vertical conception of social relations in both the social sciences and common sense. He locates morphology – the distribution of people in relation to each other – on the 'horizontal' spatial axis. Spatial distribution automatically suggests

5 Marshall (2008) provides two other points of criticism in this category. For one, he argues that the simplicity and frugality of Black's framework is deceitful. Besides, the replacement of existing validated measures pertaining to observable behaviors or opinions by new constructs concerning non-observable social phenomena ('law', 'science', 'art', 'music') which cannot be measured independent of their indicators, introduces subjectivity. In doing so, Black assumes these phenomena have an ontological status separate of human behavior without substantiating this assumption.

6 "Unlike theory which specifies sets of propositions, metaphors provide substitutes or props for the specification of relations, providing a language within which it is possible to both isolate distinguishable elements of social life and at the same time to formulate a relation between these elements" (Hunt, A. 1983: 28).

'distance', which Black broadens to 'relational distance'. Yet, although Black's conceptualization of the vertical and horizontal dimensions are not without problems,[7] they at least allow a common-sense vertical and horizontal space to be established. However, his remaining variables (culture, corporate, and normative) are defined as axes within the spatial metaphor but do not lend themselves to any geometrical location and thus the metaphor becomes more attenuated and the 'common-sense' of the metaphor is undermined. [...] On closer examination, the apparently complex pattern of variables located in social space, reduces itself as a simple linear hierarchy of several social statuses integrating income (vertical dimension), conventionality (cultural dimension), educational attainment (cultural dimension), collective action (organizational dimension) and respectability (normative dimension)." The analytical overlap between these different dimensions of social status is considerable. This may explain why one author distinguishes just two of the five dimensions (Baumgartner, M. P. 1984), while other authors use three dimensions that differ between them (Black, D. 2004, Senechal de la Roche, R. 2001), and why Black collapses the horizontal, vertical and cultural dimension when he introduces relational distance as concept (Collins, R. 2002: 657). Apparently, different dimensions can be abandoned or collapsed without cost to the integrity of the theoretical framework.

The interchangeability of the different dimensions can also be illustrated nicely by a study of Hembroff (1987) testing some of Black's hypotheses. His vignette study shows that respondents perceive theft by a drug addict who wants to finance his habit as more serious than an identical theft by a father who wants to buy medicines for his children. Hembroff attributes the different locations in social space of the drug addict and the father to the cultural dimension based on the argument that drug addicts have less conventional lifestyles than fathers have. However, in footnote ten, Hembroff refers to a reviewer suggesting it would have been better

---

7 "Black's conceptualization of the vertical dimension is problematic because he reduces the difficulties of conceptualizing social differentiation in hierarchical terms by assuming it can be captured unidimensionally by income differentiation – instead of, for example, more complex class positions. The conceptualization of the horizontal dimension is problematic, first, because it is based on the assumption that it is possible to unambiguously establish what are the center and the margin of social life. [...] Second, it is problematic to assume that intimacy – the relational distance between actors – can be separated from the self-consciousness of human beings and, without violence to its substantive content, be reduced to a behavioral and quantifiable category" (Hunt 1983: 28).

had this difference been attributed to the horizontal dimension, since drug addicts are less well integrated than fathers, while Black has connected drug use to the normative dimension arguing that drug addicts are less respectable than fathers. Not only is the analytical distinction between the dimensions unclear, it also remains undetermined how the different dimensions compare. For example, it is not clear what the theory predicts when actors occupy opposing positions on different dimensions in social space: "Who is more likely to be arrested in a police encounter, a rich hippie or a steelworker in a suit and tie?"[8] Horwitz (1983: 377) acknowledges it is problematic that the interaction between the various dimensions of social space have not been analyzed in the initial framework. The promise that future research would do so, has never really been delivered. So, conceptualizations are deficient and hypotheses underspecified.

Secondly, it is remarkable that someone who claims that quantification is the *sine qua non* of scientific inquiry relies on little quantifiable evidence and uses no form of quantitative analytical method (Frankford, D. M. 1995: 793). Behavioral sociologists indeed rely primarily on historical and anthropological studies to substantiate their claims. These qualitative methods of data collection enable the researcher to selectively look for findings confirming one's own presuppositions and to selectively ignore findings contradicting them. This is exactly what happens. Black gives numerous examples supporting his thesis that terrorism takes place between socially remote parties, while Marshall (2008) has no problem pointing out several salient counter examples of terrorism between socially close parties (e.g., Shinrikyo's attack on the Tokyo subway, the Oklahoma City bombing, Northern Ireland's 'troubles', etc.). Marshall therefore concludes: "Endlessly pointing to white swans does nothing to prove that all swans are white." The rare studies that rely on quantitative data, show mixed results at best.[9]

---

8 For example, "without a clear example of just how much distance it takes to produce terrorism, and a demonstration that the examples he counts as 'pure terrorism' do exceed it while all others do not, the ability to point to distances in one case and to closeness in another is irrelevant to the substantiation of the proposition they are enlisted to support" (Marshall, D. A. 2008: 220).

9 For example, Hembroff's (1987) findings support the predicted effects of the cultural dimension (conventionality) and the horizontal dimension (integration), but they do not support the predicted effects of the vertical and organizational dimension, and only partly support the predicted effects of the normative dimension (respectability). Kuo, S. and others (2011) conclude they have found support for the predicted effect of the vertical

In sum, it is true that, in many respects, behavioral sociology is indeed antithetical to the very same scientific values it propagates.

Purification as source of subjectivity

Besides, critics have argued that the shortcomings of behavioral sociology of law emanate directly from its aim to purify sociology. It is argued that pure sociology renders subjectivity invisible rather than eradicating it.

This mock objectivity is caused, first, by the measurement of the dependent variables law and social control (Hunt, A. 1983: 31-4). As mentioned before, Black conceives of law a quantifiable variable rather than a system of normative qualifications. "Some judgements on the quantity of law indeed have an apparent universality (e.g. an arrest is more law than no arrest). However, in most instances, we cannot assume a universal ranking: Even apparently simple quantifications of law are problematic. It appears evident that a fine of £50 is 'less law' than one of £100; but is it so self-evident? A fine of £100 on a corporation for environmental pollution is derisory and 'less' than the £50 fine imposed on a poor or unemployed person. This example shows rankings may depend entirely on *who* makes the judgement of 'seriousness'."[10] Another insurmountable problem related to the quantification of law is the incommensurability of different applications of law (Abel, R. L. 2006). "How are we to compare the amount of law applied, for example, by one officer who issues 50 speeding tickets a day with the officer who makes one homicide arrest every 3 months? [...] The general point may be made that the smaller the common-sense connection between different legal phenomena the less plausible is any attempt at rank-ordering or quantifying." In other words, "what is involved is nothing more than an act of acceptance of a common-sense social evaluation of seriousness rather than an exercise in objective quantification" (Hunt, A. 1983: 31).

Second, by taking definitions of normal and deviant behavior for granted, the complex selection and interpretation processes leading up

---

dimension, but this conclusion is based on a false interpretation of their quantitative results. They attribute the effects of gender and age to the vertical dimension, but since they have controlled for income, the effects of gender and age cannot be attributed to socio-economic status.

10 Take, for example, his assertion that "a robbery of a business is more serious than that of an individual. Property owners and judges may well regard business robbery as 'more serious', but working people would, as the literature on 'crime without victims' and crimes against organizations makes clear, probably hold the opposite view" (Hunt, A. 1983: 31).

to these definitions are rendered invisible. "Observing the ending of someone's life, for example, only becomes 'murder' if we subsequently classify this behavior as such" (Hammersley, M. 2014: 498). "A police activity is not 'legal behavior' unless we make a social attribution about the social role and normative framework within which the individual acts who is identified as 'police' by uniform, badge, etc." (Hunt, A. 1983: 24). "Indeed, Black can lucidly write about right and wrong only if he too shares the same language of right and wrong with the social actors he is describing" (Frankford, D. M. 1995: 797). "Ignoring the implicit choices underlying the processes of social ordering implies that subjectivity is rendered invisible. This is no simple failure of Black's applications but it is a consequence of the incoherence and impossibility of the methodology itself" (Hunt, A. 1983: 24).

Third, Black fails in his ambition to exclude all human motivations from his paradigm. For example, Black defines social control as the definition of and reaction to deviant behavior. In this definition, the motivation to alter this behavior is inherent.[11] "Furthermore, Black also argues that the amount of law can be measured by the tendency of people to avoid it. However, avoidance [also] necessarily embodies a direct approach to *subjective* intention" (Hunt, A. 1983: 34). In a defense of behavioral sociology, Cooney (1986: 263/4) agrees that definitions of deviant and normal behavior presuppose normative meanings shared by subjects and researchers alike and he also agrees that law and social control indeed imply intentions – avoidance of law and normalization of deviance. However, he sees no problems in focusing on the behavioral manifestations of these meanings and intentions only.[12] After agreeing that behavior is inextricably linked to meanings and intentions, Cooney (1986: 264/5) proceeds by arguing that after mapping out the behavioral referents of law and social control, predicting how they relate to social space does not have a psychological dimension to it. However, Marshall (2008: 227) convincingly argues that this impurity in the system of pure sociology not only pertains to the dependent variables – law and social control – but that the whole framework is leavened by psychological mechanisms regardless of the frantic

11 Furthermore, the different styles of social control distinguished by Black are themselves constructed upon and inseparable from conceptions of human intentions, purposes and goals (Hunt, A. 1983: 22).

12 Cooney (1986: 267, 270) upholds a moderate position, agreeing that behavioral and motivational theories can be complementary, and acknowledging that it is possible to generate useful testable propositions about social behavior that are based on motivations.

attempts to render them invisible. After all, Black argues that social locations will have an effect "to the extent that social information about the case enters the legal process, apparently meaning that actual legal actors: jurors, judges, and so on, must know about the social locations of the principals for them to have any effect." In other words, social space can only have an effect when the involved actors attribute meaning to it."

This vital issue can be illustrated by way of the law suits against O.J. Simpson, a former African American football player suspected of murder. According to Black, this case supports his ideas: O.J. Simpson was acquitted in a criminal procedure by a predominantly African American jury and he was sentenced to pay 30 million dollars in damages by a jury that had no African Americans. Black (2010: 184) points out jurors' cultural closeness to the defendant and his white victims as explanation for the difference in outcomes of both trails. Sticking to his principle to rely only on observable data, Black defines cultural closeness in terms of the skin color of the jury, victims, and defendant. Suppose we accept that skin color has indeed been decisive for the outcome in both cases – acquittal versus damages – it can only have had an impact if, consciously or subconsciously, skin color meant something to them.[13,14] Hence, the location in social space can only affect law if it is meaningful to the actors involved.

In itself it is not problematic that Black's framework is steeped with impurity. Rather, its denial and attempts to mask these impurities are problematic. Marshall believes Black gets away with this because his ideas align with common sense. "By constructing it upon the folk psychology common to most members of modern civilization, Black's system depends upon readers themselves unconsciously providing its requisite psychological underpinnings. [...] Such labor shifting typically goes unnoticed because we, like him, hold these assumptions so fundamentally that we no longer

13 Senechal de la Roche raises the question how it is possible that collective violence also occurs in tribal societies even though the relational distance between victims and perpetrators is small in these societies. Her answer is that individuals living at the brinks of a clan because of 'self-marginalization' or because they have been banned to the outskirts of a village due to their label as madmen or witches: "People may directly or indirectly distance themselves relationally, vertically, and otherwise, thereby creating the conditions for their own lynching" (Senechal de la Roche, R. 2001: 133). This exemplifies social distance can only have an effect if this is meaningful to principals.

14 Indeed, Butler (1995) has shown that minority jurors use jury nullification in cases of nonviolent conduct to alter the status quo in American criminal justice system.

recognize them as such, they are transparent to us. However, it is hard to imagine anything less scientific or more commonsensical than uncritically erecting a theory upon the foundations of ones own biases and assumptions and then denying their existence. In concealing its assumptions, a 'pure' theory maximizes the subjectivity of its formulations" (Marshall, D. A. 2008: 228/9). In sum, the ambition to purify sociology ends up in commonsense dressed up as objective science, or pseudo-science. Can the approach be saved?

WHAT IS NEEDED IS LESS PURITY RATHER THAN MORE

Are the problems connected with behavioral sociology's preoccupation with purification insurmountable or can the approach be saved by allowing impurity?

Some critics believe it is a waste of time to spend any more time and energy on behavioral sociology. However, some of its other fiercest critics argue it is with reason that behavioral sociology has so much attractive force. For example, Frankford (1995: 798, note 40) writes that Black's work is potentially important, and thus has a readership, because people can easily relate to his concepts and his categories, such as those concerning stratification and social alienation. Marshall (2008: 225) states: "One might say Black's propositions compose an unusually elaborate heuristic, a 'rule of thumb' which, based on previous experience, represents one's best first guess about how things in its realm are related. This is by no means insignificant – in abstracting and systematizing these intuitions and patterns, Black provides sociologists with a compact set of default assumptions, useful as either frames or foils for theoretical speculation and empirical testing." In other words, behavioral sociology does not have to be written off entirely. At the same time, it seems as though progress can only be made if the aspiration to purify is abandoned. Can this plea to abandon purification be contradicted?

Black's main argument against allowing unobservable behavior and motivations in the analysis is that it automatically implies values of the researcher enter the research: "[Black] somehow thinks that the reduction of law to the observable behavior of police and others, rather than a system of value statements, is necessary to eliminate the intrusion of a scientific observer's values. However, in making this claim, Black conflates the question whether the scientific observer renders her own value statements when she studies law, with the question whether law can be scientifically studied as a system of value statements" (Frankford, D. M. 1995: 792). However, value judgements and motivations can be studied value free (Hammersley, M. 2014: 498). Even Black himself agrees with this argument, as the following quote exemplifies: "Social scientists sometimes study value judgments as a form of human behaviour, such as judgments of a political or moral nature. But the study of value judgments does not require social scientists to make value judgments of their own [...]. They can study value judgments just as they study any other form of human behaviour – in a value-free fashion" (Black, D. 2013: 768). Hence, studying value judgements and motivations does not automatically jeopardizes value freedom. Moreover, allowing impurity can help tackle three problems linked to the existing version of behavioral sociology.

First, it can address the problem that behavioral sociology predicts but does not explain. Marshall (2008: 213) illustrates the crucial difference between predicting and explaining with a somewhat outdated example: the prediction that only manned cars will drive, does not explain why they drive. Explanations are indispensable for understanding why correlations exist. Behavioral sociology lacks explanations altogether because the mechanisms driving human behavior are ignored altogether.[15] Emmelman (1994: 2) raises this fundamental problem in connection to the influence of the vertical dimension in criminal law. She notices that while Black has generated a number of noteworthy propositions, "he provided no insight into the interpretive process through which social class 'causes' a greater or lesser quantity of law to be applied in legal cases." More importantly, Emmelman (1994: 1) herself offers an interpretative explanation. She demonstrates that defendant's relative social class influences the quantity of law applied to a criminal case, through actors' interpretative procedures. The attorneys' expectations of court actors shape their behavior such that lower-class defendants are likely to endure a greater quantity of law. Schwitters (2008: 121) gives explanations for the relational distance hypothesis. When the relational distance between people is small, they tend to refrain from invoking the law because they realize this can harm the relationship with their opponent outside the scope of the specific

15 Horwitz (1983: 381) also acknowledges that what was missing from Black's initial framework were mediating factors specifying the influence of the different variables.

conflict, because parties have alternative ways to influence each other's behavior, and because people want to avoid the reputational damage that the publicity of a formal legal procedure might generate for themselves. These studies prove it is possible to incorporate intentions and motivations into behavioral sociology and, hence, "to provide the bricks with which the foundations of scientific sociological theory must be laid" (Marshall, D. A. 2008: 230).[16]

A second problem that can be tackled by allowing impurity concerns the definition of social space. Above, I have argued that the different dimensions of social space are not logically derived from a general theoretical assumption, but merely consist of a set of overlapping status hierarchies. In other words, there is no theoretical necessity to always include all five dimensions in the analysis. Not always including all five dimensions of social space, on the one hand, compromises the generalizability and comparability of research findings. On the other hand, it offers the opportunity to limit the analysis to those dimensions of social space that are relevant in a particular social setting. It is logical to make the choice of which dimensions to include in the analysis depending on the meaningfulness of these dimensions in a particular setting; a strategy applied by Black (1989: 99) as well. By choosing which dimensions to include in the analysis based on their meaningfulness in a particular social context, the arbitrariness of selecting, deleting, or merging dimensions of social space can be reduced, although not eliminated. After all, there will always be a degree of arbitrariness in which dimensions are included or excluded in a particular study.

Third, allowing impurity can address the problem that is connected to Black's (2010: 185) claim that people's perceptions, thoughts, and feelings "cannot tell us what they will actually do."

---

16 Including explanations into the analysis would also enable making a comparison between Black's framework and competing theories. Black acknowledges that his predictions may be compatible with criminological theories such Hirshi's social bonds theory, Durkheim's anomy theory, and subcultural theory. However, since Black's framework consists only of predictions and lacks explanations which the competing theories do contain, the relative strength of Black's framework cannot be compared with these alternative theories. This means that while Black's framework cannot test whether the predicted patterns are spurious, the competing theories can. The fact that Black's framework cannot be falsified while the competing theories can, answers Cooney's (1986: 266) question why it would be problematic to exclude human consciousness from social theory. Moreover, including explanations would also force Black to engage in academic debate. Something Black has been blamed for avoiding more than once; Frankford, D. M. (1995: 802) "Black fails to connect his 'theory' to those of us who are engaged in a tradition of social thought," Admire, A. and Blum, D. (2015: 547) "Moral Time is not in conversation with other conflict theorists."

Instead, allegedly, like billiard balls, people are fully determined by their location in social space. This claim is irreconcilable with the practical value Black attributes to his own work. He writes: "Lawyers and law students may use this sociological knowledge. On the one hand, once lawyers start realizing that downward cases – against social inferiors – are more likely to succeed than upward cases, they may become increasingly reluctant to represent people with grievances against social superiors, or demand higher fees for doing so. Legal sociology will then become a self-fulfilling prophecy. On the other hand, because legal sociology increases the visibility of discrimination in legal life, it may provoke legal reforms to reduce discrimination" (Black, D. 1989: 95-97). Hence, Black acknowledges that the subject's ideas can both strengthen and weaken the tenability of his theoretical predictions. This is precisely the reason why scientific theories ought *not* to conform to the model of physics or chemistry in its orientation, as propagated by Black. After all, the ability to reflect upon the existing social order, to act on it, and, consequently, to have an impact on the tenability of social theories, clearly distinguishes human beings from natural phenomena (see also, Schwitters, R.J.S. 2008: 19). Allowing impurity acknowledges that people are not fully determined by their position in social space, and that their perceptions, ideas, goals, and feelings do matter (see also, Frankford, D. M. 1995).

The importance of acknowledging that unobservable behavior and motivations can in fact help us to understand what people actually do is not purely a matter of theory, but also has implications for policy-making. I can illustrate this by way of a study I have done on mandatory accident reporting at work (Mascini, P. 1998). Employees are consciously aware that accident reports may not only be used to learn from accidents and near accidents, but also to hold employees accountable for wrongful behavior. In order to avoid conflicts with colleagues whom may be held accountable for their actions leading up to accidents at work, employees are more inclined to actually report accidents and to attribute blame for negligence in their reports as the relational distance to the reportee is larger. These findings show that both punishing employees for being involved in accidents and relational closeness hamper the effectiveness of accident reporting. It would have been impossible to interpret the role of relational distance in accident reporting had I not included the meanings that employees attribute to this policy instrument. In other words, ignoring the meanings that subjects attribute to legal instruments, handicaps the policy maker in designing effective legal instruments.

Conclusion

I have come to the end of defending the first part of my thesis: behavioral sociology's ambition to purify sociology is a dead-end not only because it sins against its own scientific principles, but also because it renders subjectivity invisible rather than eradicating it. Allowing impurity would turn subjectivity into a study topic rather than denying its existence. Central research questions of impure behavioral sociology would be: What is perceived as deviant and objectionable behavior in one context and normal in another? How does social space look like in a particular context? And what reasons intermediate the impact of social space on the behavior of law? In short, allowing impurity can help transform behavioral sociology from a pseudo-science into an old-fashioned classical social theory, and can offer a way out of the blind alley this school of thought has turned into. No doubt, it is hard to conceive of any conclusion Donald Black and his followers will disagree with more wholeheartedly than this one. To me, it is the only way to keep it alive.

Behavioral law and economics

What is law and economics and why is its initial success under threat?

I now turn to the second part of my thesis. What is law and economics and why is its initial success under threat? "The seminal insight that economics provides to the analysis of law is that people respond to incentives – a generalized statement of price theory. Just as markets charge prices for commodities, laws impose sanctions on acts. To speak coherently of the legal implications of viewing law as a series of incentives, analysts have to make assumptions about the consequences of those incentives to the people subject to the legal system" (Korobkin, R. B. and Ulen, T. S. 2000: 1055). To satisfy this need, lawyer-economists imported from *rational choice theory* the assumption that individuals maximize their preferences as efficiently as possible, given existing constraints. This focus on the consequences or utility of individuals' decisions is defined as instrumental rationality (Boudon, R. 1998, 2003).

In essence, behavioral economics is defined in opposition to the assumption of the rational actor: "it is economics minus the assumption that people are rational maximizers of their satisfaction" (Posner, R. A. 1998: 1552). Oddly enough though, behavioral economists continue to use instrumental rationality as their main point of reference. They commonly refer to 'bounded rationality', 'bounded will-power', and 'bounded self-interest'. This suggests, although bounded, that instrumental rationality is still the standard. In this sense, Kelman (1998: 1580) is right in stating that behavioral economics and rational choice theory stand together in "irreconcilable mutual dependence", "bound together in a form of rhetorical duet or ritualized dance."

This means that, on the one hand, the behavioral economics movement has criticized the assumption of the rational actor in legal analysis. On the other hand, it has treated other types of behavior than instrumental rationality as a residual category. For this reason, I will use the typology of human behavior introduced by the sociologist Max Weber (1925). His typology allows each of the different types of behavior to be distinguished analytically. Besides instrumental rationality, Weber distinguishes traditional and affective behavior, and substantive rationality. "Affective behavior is infused by emotion, and enacted without premeditation. Traditional behavior originates from prevailing habits that are internalized to such extent that an individual no longer realizes why she always performs the same actions under certain circumstances. As is the case with affective behavior, there is no premeditation about the potential consequences or utility of the act. Substantive rationality arises from the conviction that a certain action possesses intrinsic value ('*Eigenwert*'), independent of utility or result. Executing the act is the goal in itself. The captain who is convinced that she owes it to her honor to jump a sinking ship last, behaves substantively rational. When she would abuse her authority to be the first to enter a rescue boat, others would see her as a woman without honor. And this knowledge would be unbearable" (De Jong, M. 1997: 116).

While law and economics starts from the assumption that individuals make instrumentally rational decisions, studies in behavioral economics have tried to show that the functioning of the law cannot be well understood based on this assumption and that policy recommendations based on this assumption are likely to be flawed. I will classify this research in terms of Max Weber's typology of human behavior in order to show that the three other types of behavior are indispensable to understand the functioning of the law, and that policy recommendations can be derived from these insights. I will discuss the criticism and recommendations per type of behavior.

EXPOSING THE LIMITATIONS OF THE RATIONAL ACTOR

Emotions. "Scholars have begun to discuss the role of emotions in legal discourse by addressing the 'appropriateness' of various emotions for the substantive law, or by attempting to model the place of emotions in the law" (Blumenthal, J. A. 2005). In principle, emotions have no place in the concept of the rational decision-maker. "Yet, some rational choice scholars have attempted to explicitly reconcile emotion with rational decision-making by incorporating emotional states into such decision processes. Running through such discussions of emotion is the implicit (and at times explicit) assumption that emotional states are conscious and controllable, that people are aware of and can predict their emotions, and that as a partial result, 'people can cultivate their emotions'" (Blumenthal, J. A. 2005). The assumptions that people are able to predict and control their emotions have both proven problematic.

First, "substantial empirical evidence demonstrates that although people are relatively adept at knowing which emotion they will experience and whether it will be positive or negative, people are surprisingly inaccurate at predicting the intensity and the duration of those emotions" (Blumenthal, J. A. 2005: 167). [...] For instance, although any traumatic experience is harrowing and painful, through a process of 'hedonic adaptation', victims of such negative experiences are able to return to a more normal experience of emotion sooner than might be expected. [...] This inability to accurately predict future emotional states implicates, for example, a fundamental aspect of the civil jury system – the assessment of damage awards for noneconomic losses such as 'pain and suffering', 'mental anguish', or 'loss of (or 'lost') enjoyment of life'. [...] In order to compensate a tort victim for the distress she is reasonably anticipated to suffer in the future, prospective damages may sometimes be awarded. [...] If jurors consistently over predict the degree of emotional distress a victim will suffer, damage awards will be inflated and victims will be overcompensated" (Blumenthal, J. A. 2005: 183).

Second, research has demonstrated that people are limited in their ability to control their emotions. "As emotions intensify, they exert an ever-increasing influence on behavior. Indeed, at sufficient levels of intensity, emotions can overwhelm cognitive processing altogether. Under the influence of intense emotions, people often report themselves as being (or having been) 'out of control' or 'acting against their own self-interest'" (Mitchell, G. 2002: note 95). For example, "anger or pride may lead to increased frequencies of trials, depending in part on parties' beliefs and expectations about the other party's behavior, beliefs, and emotions. [...] For instance, a plaintiff 'outraged by an unexpected tort would bring suit even when that suit has negative expected wealth value,' but she 'would not bring suit if that tort had been expected'" (Blumenthal, J. A. 2005: 205). The consequence of this is more trials than would be predicted by the rational choice model, unless steps are taken to mitigate the parties' evaluative biases.

Taking into account people's limited abilities to predict and control emotions has two potential implications for legal policymakers. First, "one way to address some of the concerns related to the limited ability to predict emotions would be to admit expert evidence on affective forecasting research, as well as coping mechanisms more generally, during the damages phase of civil trials that involve damages for emotional distress" (Blumenthal, J. A. 2005: 187). Second, the importance of emotions for subject's to the law, provides support for alternative forms of dispute resolution allowing litigants room to ventilate and deal with their own emotions and with the emotions of their opponents. This is congruent with the modern trend in civil litigation toward mandatory settlement conferences, court-ordered mediation, and nonbinding arbitration.

Tradition. "The importance of traditional behavior for legal scholarship is exemplified by research showing that past behaviors can affect current choices. [...] Because economists employing rational choice theory generally assume preferences are determined independent of behaviors, a common assumption is that choices an actor has made in the past will not affect his current preference structure. [...] To the extent that rational choice theorists believe that yesterday's choice will affect today's, the correlation is usually presumed to be negative, an application of the concept of declining marginal utility. [...] The problem for the conventional conceptions of rational choice theory is that the relationship between past and present actions is often positive rather than negative. That is, the fact that an actor acted in a certain way in the past can increase the likelihood that he will act in the same way in the future" (Korobkin, R. B. and Ulen, T. S. 2000: 1114).

This positive effect of past choices on current ones can result, among others, from people's habit to simplify their tasks by using rules of thumb, or heuristics. "For example, judges reason by reference to past cases; jury judgements about damage awards are likely to be based on anchors, even arbitrary ones, such as the plaintiff demand; and people tend to think that events are more likely if an example is readily called to mind or 'available'. Consequently, media coverage of major incidents fuels demand for risk regulation" (Jolls, C., Sunstein, C. R. and Thaler, R. 1998). As a result of these heuristics, cases are not entirely evaluated based on their own merits, but are connected to regular behavioral patterns or with what is consciously or unconsciously conceived of as familiar and self-evident. The same applies to a number of biases unraveled by behavioral economists. For instance, the so-called 'confirmation bias' shows that individuals are inclined to decide based on information that confirm already existing ideas, and to ignore contradicting evidence. The confirmation bias can result, for instance, in miscarriages of justice because prosecutors end up with tunnel vision. Furthermore, the 'hindsight bias' shows that "people often think, in hindsight, that things that happened were inevitable, or nearly so. The resulting 'hindsight bias' can much distort legal judgement. For example, judgements about whether someone was negligent may well be affected by this bias; if a bad outcome occurred juries are likely to believe that it was inevitable. For decision makers prone to hindsight bias, the line between strict liability and negligence may be quite thin" (Sunstein, C. R. 1999: 138).

"Acknowledging the positive relationship between past and present behaviors, has two potentially broad implications for legal policy. The first, and relatively uncontroversial, implication is that policymakers attempting to encourage or discourage certain behavior should realize that behaviors motivated by tradition are likely to be much more difficult to manipulate than rational choice theory would predict. When past behavior, rather than merely inherent value, drives the utility that an actor receives from current behavior, laws that try to offset the inherent utility of a behavior with corresponding costs will not create a sufficient deterrence. The more controversial policy question is to what extent the law should paternalistically attempt to protect individuals from 'harmful' habits, traditions, and addictions (those that reduce an actor's total utility over time), or to encourage 'beneficial' habits, traditions, and addictions (those that increase future utility)" (Korobkin, R. B. and Ulen, T. S. 2000: 1116).

Substantive rational behavior. A trite but nonetheless highly relevant finding for legal scholarship is that under certain conditions individuals subordinate their self-interest to compliance with social norms. Apparently, this contradicts a version or rational choice theory that assumes individuals act selfishly.

According to rational choice theory, the more the risks of being penalized for violating laws exceed the benefits of doing so, the more individuals are inclined to comply. In a review article, Robbennolt (2015) confirms that financial incentives influence the inclination to behave unethically, but she also concludes that individuals value their moral self-image and that this concern moderates other incentives for unethical behavior. "Thus, even when there are financial incentives for deviant behavior and there is little or no chance of being caught, not everyone violates rules, and those who do tend only to do so a little bit. [...] Social proof and social norms act to influence people's sense of what behavior is appropriate within a setting. Individuals look to others to figure out how to behave and to understand the relevant social norms in a situation, particularly in ambiguous circumstances.[17] [...] The effect of peer behavior on a decision maker's own ethical behavior is strengthened when the peer is a member of the individual's in-group or when there is otherwise a feeling of social closeness with that peer. [...] Finally, beyond the social influence of observing and talking with colleagues and others, ethical influence may come in the form of direction from an authority figure" (Robbennolt, J. K. 2015: 81). In sum, there are many situations in which individuals do things or abstain from them because they deem this morally right, or because

17 "They may conform their own behavior to the behavior of others; they learn vicariously through the experiences, rewards, and punishments of others; and they engage in social comparison processes. And, indeed, decision makers are more likely to act unethically when peers, colleagues, and others around them act unethically. The stories that are told and the conversations that colleagues have about ethics can also shape group norms. Following moral conversations, for example, people tend to act more ethically than they do following more self-interested dialog" (Robbennolt, J. K. 2015: 81).

they believe this is expected of them, independent of the utility or results of this behavior in terms of self-interest.

"When individual behavior motivated by social norms differs from what would be in the actors' direct self-interest, there are a number of potential implications for legal policymakers. First, the existence of a social norm supporting or undermining a particular desired behavior can affect whether and to what extent policymakers need to employ law to encourage the behavior. In other words, law might be used to encourage individuals to violate inefficient or undesirable social norms or may support existing social norms. [...] Second, rather than attempting to support or impede social norms, policymakers might attempt to shape social norms through law and other forms of public policy. [...] For example, by banning the selling of babies, the selling of bodily organs, or the selling of sex, the government might reinforce a social norm that neither the body nor its parts should be commodified. [...] Third, the existence of a norm favoring a certain behavior might be evidence that this particular behavior is more efficient than alternatives, or at least more efficient than alternatives that are likely to be encouraged by lawmakers engaged in political decision-making. Unless they have a clear reason to believe a prevailing norm is not efficient, legal policymakers might be wise not to interfere with the norm. This principle of non-interference can be operationalized by lawmakers either not legislating in a given field, thus relying on norms to be self-enforcing, or by codifying the prevailing norms, thus supporting the prevailing norms with the enforcement power of the state" (Korobkin, R. B. and Ulen, T. S. 2000: 1133).

CONCLUSION

While law and economics starts from the assumption that individuals make instrumentally rational decisions, Max Weber's typology of human behavior can be used to show that empirical studies in behavioral economics have tried to show that the functioning of the law cannot be understood well without taking into account the three other types of behavior. As such, the attack on the assumption of the rational actor can be conceived of as a plea for introducing impurity into law and economics. How has law and economics responded to this attack? Basically, two responses can be distinguished: one denouncing the behavioral economics movement, and one embracing it.

WITHERING THE ASSUMPTION OF THE RATIONAL ACTOR?

DENOUNCING BEHAVIORAL ECONOMICS

The proponents of the defensive response claim that the limitations attributed to rational choice theory are grossly exaggerated. Their main argument is that the actions that appear to be non-instrumental – tradition, emotion, and substantive rationality – are actually instrumental *at a deeper level* (Boudon, R. 1998: 818). This conversion from non-instrumental to instrumental is obtained by introducing the postulate that, contrary to appearances, actions are the product of self-interest. Richard Posner (1998), one of the founding fathers of law and economics, is a clear representative of this argumentation, at least in his earlier publications (for a more moderate version of this position, see Faure, M. G. 2009).

Posner conceives of emotional behavior as part of instrumental rationality rather than as an independent behavioral type. He argues "that preferences cannot be divorced from emotion, or emotion from their stimuli, and so instrumental reasoning cannot be thought pervaded with irrationality merely because a frequent goal of such reasoning is a preference that we would not have if we were not emotional beings" (Posner, R. A. 1998: 1554). Based on this argument he defends rational choice theory against the outcomes of so-called 'ultimatum games'. In ultimatum games, donors are given a money amount and are asked to allocate a share of the amount that they are given to their recipient. If the recipient accepts the share, then both donor and recipient go home with these respective allocations, but if the recipient declines then both parties go home with nothing. The finding that recipients usually prefer to remain empty handed rather than to accept a derisory offer questions the assumption of the rational actor. After all, for a rational actor, anything is better than nothing. Posner rebuts by arguing that refusing insultingly low offers can be interpreted in terms of a remnant of adaptive evolutionary behavior. After all, "[i]nability to make a credible threat to retaliate renders a person virtually defenseless in a prelegal, prepolitical society" (Posner, R. A. 1998: 1562). Finding the courage to retaliate would require a state of emotional arousal. Allegedly, the emotions connected to the ingrained inclination to retaliate causes recipients to decline insultingly low offers in ultimatum games. [Thus] "having an unshakable commitment to retaliate may be ex ante rational by lowering the risk of being a victim of aggression, even though, if the risk materializes, acting on the commitment will then (that is, ex post) become irrational. [This means] the response of turning down an insultingly low offer in an ultimate game is in a narrow sense emotional rather than rational, but in a broader sense rational because the emotion that generates it is part of a cognitive emotional complex that enables the making of commitments that are rational ex ante" (Posner, R. A. 1998: 1565).

In relation to traditional behavior, Posner argues that some critics still attribute to rational choice theory the assumption that individuals decide based on complete information. However, he believes this assumption has long been aborted by rational choice theory. Precisely because collecting information is expensive, it is efficient to resort to rules of thumb. This explains why the fact that an actor acted in a certain way in the past often increases the likelihood that he will act in the same way in the future. As such, for example, the availability bias – the propensity to overestimate the relevance of salient or memorable incidents at the expense of the accurate prediction of the probability of future events – can be conceived of a rational reduction of complexity and uncertainty. Absent of other information, it is smart to trust in indirect signals such as the availability of salient or memorable incidents. For the same reason it is also rational to adjust one's own behavior to that of others. "Habit-formation is [simply] one way in which 'learning by doing' works; tasks are performed more quickly and with less effort when they become habitual" (Posner, R. A. 1998: 1567). In other words, traditional behavior is a means to make efficient choices and to reduce complexity and uncertainty.

Posner (1998: 1561) reduces substantive rational behavior to instrumental rationality by falling back on evolutionary biology again. He writes: "Evolutionary biology sees altruism as a trait that promotes inclusive fitness, defined as maximizing the number of copies of one's genes by maximizing the number of creatures carrying them, weighted by the closeness of the relation. The inclusive fitness of a social animal like man is greatly enhanced by his having a proclivity to help his relatives, and so it is plausible to suppose that this proclivity evolved as an adaptive mechanism. [...] Nowadays we interact a great deal with strangers. But our instincts are easily fooled when confronted with conditions to which human beings never had a chance to adapt biologically. [...] Voting, giving to charities, and refraining from littering, in circumstances in which there is neither visible reward for these cooperative behaviors nor visible sanctions for defection, may illustrate an instinctual, and as it were biologically mistaken, generalization of cooperation from small-group interactions, in which altruism is rewarded (hence reciprocal) and failures to reciprocate punished, to large-group interactions in which the prospects of reward and punishment are so slight that cooperation ceases to be rational. [...] We can see how bringing evolutionary biology into the picture enables the concept of rationality to be enlarged to cover phenomena [such as altruism and fairness] that [Jolls, Sunstein, and Thaler] classify as irrational.

In short, many findings put forward by behavioral economics with the aim to criticize the assumed rational actor, instead are treated as confirmations of the very same rational actor by Posner. Nonetheless, he realizes that doing so is risky when he writes: “Of course, enriching the rational-choice model runs a risk of explaining nothing by explaining everything.” (Posner, R. A. 1998: 1567). This remark is spot on, even though Posner does not elaborate what this risk entails. I will do that for him.

First, ‘enriching’ rational choice theory implies that the concept of instrumental rationality is stretched to such extent that it can no longer be distinguished from other types of behavior. Where does instrumental rationality start, and where do emotions, traditions, and substantive rationality end? Furthermore, underlying Posner’s argument is the assumption that the three other types of behavior merely support instrumental rationality. He altogether overlooks the possibility that the reverse may be true, without substantiating his ranking order anywhere.[18] This suggests his assumed ranking order is based on nothing else than the wish to uphold instrumental rationality as the ultimate type of behavior (Jolls, C., Sunstein, C. R. and Thaler, R. 1998: 1593/4).

One way to refute this criticism of overstretching the concept of instrumental rationality is by treating the causes of behavior, by principle, as unknowable (Boudon, R. 1998: 819). Based on this positivist epistemology, reasons are unknowable, hence researchers

18 For example, it is more plausible to assume that emotions dominate rationality than to assume the reverse. What human beings reflect upon and think about is emotionally loaded. Neuro physiologically, all information first passes the emotional part of the brains, and only subsequently, after being emotionally loaded, information enters the parts of the brains that execute planning, mental imagination etc. The connections from the emotion parts of the brains to the ratio parts of the brains are more extensive and faster than are the reverse connections (Weenink, D. 2009).

can only rely on observable human behavior, or what economists designate as revealed preferences (see also Schroeder, J. 2001). Posner indeed argues that the only thing that matters is whether or not theories incorporating this postulate reproduce correctly in the observed data (Jolls, C., Sunstein, C. R. and Thaler, R. 1998: 1599).[19] Posner's argument renders the reasons people give for their own actions as completely irrelevant. For example, if a player in an ultimatum game indicates that the only reason for rejecting a derisory offer was pure indignation or the definite conviction that the offer was principally unfair, then Posner knows it was 'really' because she did not want to give the impression to her opponent she was weak. "However, at this point, the rational choice theorist should explain the 'false consciousness' she attributes to the actor." Why does the subject think she acted out of emotion, habit, or conviction while she *really* did for instrumental reasons? "The reluctance to take subjective factors into account because the causes of behavior are unknowable is unfounded. After all, I can check what motivates someone's behavior. Even if I cannot perceive directly her reasons, I can reconstruct them. This reconstruction has the status of a theory that can be confronted with data. That the reasons motivating people are not directly observable does not imply that their reconstruction is doomed to be arbitrary" (Boudon, R. 1998: 819). In other words, although the reasons motivating people cannot be observed directly, it is still problematic to attribute motives to people they cannot identify with.

A second problem connected to ignoring reasons motivating actions is that this renders it possible to define completely opposing behaviors as instrumentally rational. This problem is present, for example, in relation to behavioral studies showing people's leaning to attribute more importance to losses than to gains. Whereas Posner attributes loss aversion to an profitable evolutionary survival mechanism, there is a long tradition in economics of arguing that competition or evolution will drive out precisely those people who show loss aversions because they do not do what they are supposed to as rational actors. After all, standard reasoning in economics is that it is rational to ignore sunk costs meaning that irreversible past

19 It is ironic that Friedman and Posner take a theory rooted in a radical individualistic philosophy and a desire to understand human behavior and purport to remove individual psychology from it (Schroeder, J. 2001).

actions should not influence current choices. This means, both loss aversion and its absence can be interpreted in terms of adaptive evolutionary behavior. "It is difficult to see what conclusions should be drawn from the fact that evolution can be shown to produce a behavior – loss aversion – and the absence of that behavior" (Jolls, C., Sunstein, C. R. and Thaler, R. 1998: 1600). In fact, resorting to revealed preferences makes rational choice theory incapable of generating predictions at all because whatever happens can be said to have been a result of the relevant utility function, constructed ex post (Schroeder, J. 2001, Arcuri, A. 2008). Such post hoc explanations do not help the policy-maker who wants to know beforehand what is to be expected from legal instruments, and who will not be interested in what an instrumentally rational actor would do, knowing such an actor does not exist in many situations (Korobkin, R. B. and Ulen, T. S. 2000).[20]

A third problem connected to the attempt to conceive of other types of behavior as instrumental rationality at a deeper level, is that is requires auxiliary assumptions to do so. Posner argues that altruistic behavior that does not serve a foreseeable self-interest is to be seen as a residual of biological instincts once needed to pass on one's own genes and reproduce. Nowhere does Posner substantiate the claim that misguided instincts steer our behavior. Not even does he clarify how this claim can be tested at all (Jolls, C., Sunstein, C. R. and Thaler, R. 1998).[21] On top of that, it is superfluous to make this additional claim. "Behavior that has survived the test of time may or may not have a lot to do with biology, and while it would be interesting (and in some ways potentially valuable) to know, a behavioral approach to the economic analysis of law can proceed whether or not the evolutionary account is right" (Jolls, C.,

20 In another example, Korobkin, R. B. and Ulen, T. S. (2000: 1065/6) state that "Unfortunately, expanding the conception of 'self-interest' to include other-regarding preferences in addition to selfish ones would rob the notion of 'self-interest' of all of its predictive value. We would no longer be able to predict that people would litter if doing so risks no punishment, or that products would be more dangerous without products liability law, because people walking in the park may or may not gain utility from keeping the park tidy for their neighbors, and manufacturers may or may not gain utility from preventing harm to their customers."

21 Posner suggest there is more overlap between evolutionary biology and law and economics than is justified: "evolutionary psychology seems even more committed than law and economics to the idea (wrongly associated with Coase) that legislation or legal change is futile as an instrument of social progress. The two disagree on money versus reproductive fitness as the primary motive for human action. Law and economics focuses on the present and is especially weak when it has to explain circumstances that change over time; evolutionary psychology focuses on the distant past" (Bernstein, A. 2005: note 117).

Sunstein, C. R. and Thaler, R. 1998: 1600).[22] What is also problematic is that the hypothesis that dysfunctional instincts continue to steer behavior contradicts Posner's own optimism "that people can be cured of some of the cognitive quirks and weakness of will with biological roots" (Posner, R. A. 1998: 1575). After all, if people can unlearn behavior which prevents them from acting rationally with no offsetting gains, why then do they continue to show it when it comes to altruism or fairness?

In short, the assumption of the rational actor underlying rational choice theory can only be upheld by stretching the concept of instrumental rationality so far that it can no longer be distinguished from other types of behavior, by ignoring reasons motivating people's behavior, and by using post hoc explanations.

EMBRACING BEHAVIORAL ECONOMICS

There are other lawyer-economists who welcome behavioral economics, by taking the limitations of the rational actor seriously. This welcoming approach focuses on the finding that individuals sometimes obey social norms that are contrary to their direct self-interests (for example, Ellickson 1989, Cooter, R. 1995, Rostain, T. 2000, Faure, M. G. 2009). Representatives of this position deem attempts insufficient to interpret such behavior in terms of instrumental rationality at a deeper level.

One can argue that people voluntarily comply to social norms because they want to avoid informal sanctions and because they expect to be rewarded with esteem and recognition if they do so. However, subsequently, this argument raises the question as to why

22 There are indeed theories available that explain other directed behavior without reverting to an alleged evolutionary origin. For example, restorative justice and reintegrative shaming suffice with the assumption that social acceptance is a basic human need, without retracing this need to an evolutionary origin (Brennan, G. and Pettit, P. 2004; Mascini, P. 2016). From this assumption is derived the hypothesis that people are inclined to comply because they care about what others think of them. Allegedly, deviating from social norms brings forth feelings of shame and guilt. The assumed importance of the need for social acceptance as a compliance motive is underscored by the theoretical argument that restorative justice and reintegrative shaming are most likely to spur on feelings of guilt and shame in close-knit communities. Allegedly, the more interdependent a community is, the more individuals care about other people's opinion of them. The assumed importance of the need for social acceptance as a compliance motive is also expressed by the expectation that gossiping – confirming social norms by expressing disapproval of deviance committed by others – has a positive impact on compliance. Supposedly, gossiping induces feelings of guilt and shame and, consequently, increases the inclination to comply.

individuals care to make the effort to punish deviance even though punishing can be costly. "After all, punishing someone for violating a social norm carries a risk of retaliation by the sanction's target. A rational actor would prefer to free-ride on the punishments meted out by others rather than to bear the cost of imposing the sanction herself." Again, one could argue that individuals are prepared to sanction because they may expect a reward for doing so. However, logically one ends up at the question of why this precise behavior is rewarded, rather than, for example, encouraging the violation of a social norm. "Even if the motivation to sanction a norm violator might be explained by external incentives – people think highly of people who informally sanction others for violating norms – the motivation for expressing such approval cannot, in turn, be reduced to external incentives. The intellectual problem of unselfish behavior, solved on the level of primary norm enforcement, reemerges at the next level, or, if solved on the secondary level, at the next level after that" (Elster 1989 cited by Rostain, T. 2000: 992).

According to Cooter (1995), this conundrum cannot be solved by conceiving preferences as given, as is custom in rational choice theory. Preferences themselves require explanation. Supposedly, individuals may choose to act unselfishly, because of who they want to be. By internalizing values connected to impersonal roles, the gap between the self-interest of the agent and the interest of the principal reduces, rendering external control superfluous. Internalizing makes sure someone adopts shared norms to such an extent that it becomes part of one's self-image. When that happens, a distinction arises between two types of self-interest. A thin version looks only to objective payoffs in wealth or power. A thick version modifies objective payoffs to encompass the subjective value of morality. When actors decide based on a thick self, the cost of violating social norms is not loss of esteem in the eyes of peers but guilt or shame for doing something the actor experiences as 'wrong'. The costs of violating social norms are imposed not by society but by the violator herself.[23]

23 In commenting on a previous draft of this text, Don Weenink rightfully wrote "that a thick self can only become thick with morality after having been exposed to groups in which this morality was developed/celebrated/enacted and internalized later (an emotional process, morality is emotional, as is value rationality: it feels bad to violate it, it feels good to uphold it). What feels so wrong is a failure to comply to one's very own principles. But eventually, these principles are social, imposed by groups. So the distinction between costs of violating social norms imposed by society and by the violator herself is not a real distinction. It is 'society' or rather group morality in us."

Cooter and others do not believe that distinguishing between a thin and a thick self, or between egoism and altruism, has huge consequences for rational choice theory. Supposedly, incremental adaptations inside the rational actor paradigm suffice. What is more, incorporating the conceptions of a thick self and of altruism in rational choice theory would even hold the prospect of developing a general theory of social behavior. However, the more fundamental the distinction between these types of behaviors is, the more problematic it becomes, first, to assume that it is instrumental rationality which steers individual behavior. After all, acknowledging the existence of a thick self and of altruism imply that substantive rationality can also steer individuals' behavior. Second, acknowledging the existence of these types of behavior raises the question under which conditions the thin or the thick self, or egoism or altruism prevails. Precisely because rational choice theory starts from the assumption of the rational actor, this crucial question cannot be raised in this paradigm (see also Schroeder, J. 2001). In other words, the more fundamental the distinction between instrumental rationality and substantive rationality is, the more fundamentally the rational choice paradigm is challenged.

Cooter himself in fact already recognizes that the distinction between a thin and a thick self is crucial, by admitting both selves can be incompatible. Lindenbergh and Mascini (2013) have empirically demonstrated they can indeed be incompatible, by studying how victims of personal injuries attempt to satisfy their concomitant need for financial compensation and restoration of a harmed relationship with the injurer. The attempt to fulfil both needs confronts victims with a double dilemma: on the one hand, a calculative attitude of the victim increases the chance of receiving a good financial compensation, while at the same time it hampers reconciliation with the injurer. On the other hand, forgiveness promotes restoration of the distorted relationship with the injurer, but at the same time involves the risk of an injurer deploying excuses and admission of guilt in an attempt to lower damages. This double dilemma generates a game situation in which both the weighing of the self-interest and the mutual interest by the victim and the weighing of both types of interests attributed to the injurer may vary. "Once we recognize social interactions as potentially exhibiting a variety of game structures, we must acknowledge that a mix of motives operates in human behavior, including cooperation, altruism, and self-interest" (Little 1991: 65 cited by Rostain 2000: 999-1000).

This theoretical matter also has implications for policy making. Perhaps the most important implication is that laws that try to offset the inherent utility of non-compliant behavior with corresponding costs may crowd out substantive rational behavior. Studies have shown, for example, that people are more inclined to comply with environmental rules when *no* sanctions are attached to rule violations than when there is the prospect of a small sanction (Tenbrunsel, A. E. and Messick, D. M. 1999), the introduction of small fines for the delay in collecting children from school actually produces more, not less, in the way of lateness (Sunstein, C. R. 1999: 129), and people accept the presence of nuclear waste on their city's land more easily when they are *not* offered compensation than when they are (Frey, B. S. 1997). What explains these findings is that the presence of a system of rewards and punishments signals that individuals are expected to make a cost-benefit analysis, while the absence of such incentives appeals to moral and ethical reasoning. This shows that, under certain circumstances, it can be counterproductive to design legal instruments based on the assumption that individuals act instrumentally rational.

In short, lawyer-economists whom welcome behavioral economics wrongfully assume that distinguishing between a thin and a thick self, or between egoism and altruism, can easily be reconciled with rational choice theory. After all, precisely the fact that these distinctions imply that substantial rationality and instrumental rationality have to be taken equally seriously as guiding principles of behavior, proves it is problematic to assume it is instrumental rationality that steers behavior and to take preferences for granted. In other words, recognizing the importance of these distinctions automatically implies that two pillars underlying rational choice theory fail. Consequently, the hope that rational choice theory can come up with an integrative theory of social action disappears beyond the horizon.

CONCLUSION

I have taken issue with the goal of scientific purity in the behavioral study of law, conceived as the deliberate choice to postulate a limited number of universally applicable behavioral principles. In connection with behavioral sociology, I have argued that attempts to objectify law makes the subjective choices underpinning this process invisible. Furthermore, that deliberately overlooking the motivations that drive people's behavior renders the approach meaningless. In relation to law and economics, I have argued that the assumption of the rational actor can only be saved by stretching the concept of instrumental rationality so far that it can no longer be distinguished from other types of behavior, by ignoring the reasons people give for their own actions, and by using post hoc explanations. Moreover, I have argued that acknowledging the importance of other types of behavior than instrumental rationality is incompatible with rational choice theory.

While behavioral sociology is a school of thought that has pretty much turned into itself, behavioral economics has made sure this is no longer the case for law and economics. By delivering empirically founded criticism on the assumption that individuals act rationally, lawyer-economists have been pressed hard to critically assess the suitability of the general assumptions underlying rational choice theory. It has made at least part of the lawyer-economists to open up, expand, and stretch. Consequently, the boundaries between law and economics and behavioral economics have blurred (Bernstein, A. 2005: 132). It is difficult to overestimate the value of this achievement by behavioral law.

At the same time, the empirical approach of behavioral economics is not beatific. For one, empirical research will not be able to solve all scientific disputes. "Ultimately, the choice of behavioral assumptions to guide policy will depend to some extent on value preferences and unrealistic or untestable assumptions about human nature, because while empirical research can provide better answers than we currently have, it will not provide incontestable or simple answers about legal rationality for prescriptive use" (Mitchell, G. 2002: 76/7). For example, Posner (1998: 1559) probably has a point arguing that underlying behavioral economics is "the implicit *liberal* conception of the average person – good, but inept, and for both reasons not very responsive to incentives, though perhaps rather plastic. The implicit *conservative* view of the average person, in contrast, is that he is competent but bad; hence conservatives emphasize incentives and constraints." To a certain extent, these ideological views may influence the scientific study of the law as well. In other words, empirical behavioral research is a necessary but insufficient condition for critically assessing the assumptions underlying one's own research and one's policy recommendations.

Furthermore, there are indications that some behavioral economists replace the problematic assumption of the rational actor by equally problematic psychological claims. The literature is riddled by statements such as 'people are loss averse' or 'people suffer from over optimism'. However, "behavioral decision theorists have yet to discover the decontextualized, universal psychological processes of judgment and decision-making that are implied by such statements" (Mitchell, G. 2002: 125). Therefore, "behavioralists need to realize that the sensitivity of legal cognition to personal and situational characteristics render the development of a general model of legal behavior that is both reasonably descriptive and parsimonious unlikely" (Mitchell, G. 2002: 130, see also Korobkin, R. B. and Ulen, T. S. 2000, Rostain, T. 2000).

This implies that although the behavioral economics movement has opened up the road heading towards impurity, this road must be pursued even further. First, by acknowledging that behavioral responses to law depend essentially on the meaningful interaction of individuals with their environment. This implies legal instruments need to be tailored to the specificities of the contexts in which they are applied. Although such a contingency approach "may complicate theory and research, its endorsement recognizes the impropriety of sweeping statements about the nature of legal judgment and decision-making" (Mitchell, G. 2002: 130).

Second, studies in behavioral law have convincingly shown that all four types of behavior that have been discussed here contribute to the functioning of the law, often in different combinations. Yet until now, even in behavioral economics, instrumental rationality has remained the natural point of reference by focusing on its boundaries. The emancipation from law and economics can be continued by replacing the conception of '*bounded*' rationality by that of '*situated*' rationality (Hawkins, K. 2001). Whether driven by emotions, traditions, instrumentality, or moral convictions, usually it is possible to understand how people behave in a particular situation and why. "The behavioral researcher is well advised to look carefully at his or her research participant's behavior, beliefs, and goals to discern 'the method in the apparent madness'" (Mitchell, G. 2002: note 121). Trying to understand what motivates people's behavior, also automatically implies it is insufficient to take observable behavior for granted. After all, the meanings of observable behavior do not speak for themselves.

Taking seriously the meanings of people's behavior also implies that mathematical models and experiments will not suffice as research methods. "In contrast to proof in the context of a more behaviorist hypothesis or a rational choice hypothesis, proving social meaning traditionally involves offering a rich contextual analysis of multiple meanings and counter meanings, and that is based on in-depth knowledge acquired through intensive interviewing, participating, observing, and exploring by detached researchers, corroborated as much as possible by experimental and statistical analyses" (Harcourt, B. E. 2000, see also Arcuri, A. 2008). So, using situated rationality as the starting point in the study of law also demands pluralism of methods.

To sum up, I propose to replace behavioral sciences of law by an approach that not only takes empirical research seriously, but also adopts a modest attitude by surrendering the ambition to come up with universally applicable predictions and by taking seriously meaningful behavior.

Ik heb gezegd.

Acknowledgements

I would like to thank Michael Faure, Dick Houtman, Rob Schwitters, and Don Weenink for their many useful and constructive comments on previous versions of this text.

Literature

Abel RL, 'General Damages Are Incoherent, Incalculable, Incommensurable, and Inegalitarian (But Otherwise a Great Idea' (2006) 55 DePaul Law Review 253.

Admire A and Blum D, 'Moral Time. By Donald Black. New York: Oxford University Press, 2011, 288 (Book review)' (2015) 49(2) Law & Society Review 546.

Arcuri A, 'Eclecticism in Law and Economics' (2008) 1(3) Erasmus Law Review 59.

Baumgartner MP, 'Social Control from Below' in Black, Donald (ed), *Toward a General Theory of Social Control* (Academic Press, Inc. 1984).

Bernstein A, 'Whatever Happened to Law and Economics?' (2005) 64 Maryland Law Review 101.

Black D, *The Behavior of Law* (Academic Press 1976).
–'Crime as Social Control' (1983) 48(February) American Sociological Review 34.
–*Sociological Justice* (Oxford University Press 1989).
–*The Social Structure of Right and Wrong* (Academic Press 1993).
–'The Epistemology of Pure Sociology' (1995) 20(3) Law & Social Inquiry 829.
–'The Purification of Sociology' (2000a) 31(6) Contemporary Sociology 704.
–'Dreams of Pure Sociology' (2000b) 18(3) Sociological Theory 343.
–'The Geometry of Terrorism' (2004) 22(1, March) Sociological Theory 14.
–'How Law Behaves. An Interview with Donald Black' in *The Behavior of Law: Special Edition* (Emerald 2010).
–*Moral Time* (Oxford University Press 2011).
–'On the Almost Inconceivable Misunderstandings Concerning the Subject of Value-Free Science' (2013) 64(4) The British Journal of Sociology 763.
Blumenthal JA, 'Law and the Emotions: The Problems of Affective Forecasting' (2005) 80 Indiana Law Journal 155.
Boudon R, 'Limitations of Rational Choice Theory' (1998) 104(3) American Journal of Sociology 817.
–'Beyond Rational Choice Theory' (2003) 29 Annual Review of Sociology 1.
Brennan G and Pettit P, *The Economy of Esteem: An Essay on Civil and Political Society* (Oxford University Press 2004).
Butler P, 'Racially Based Jury Nullification: Black Power in the Criminal Justice System' (1995) 105 Yale Law Journal 677.
Collins R, 'Black's Contributions to a General Theory of Conflict' (2002) 31(6) Contemporary Sociology 655.
Cooney M, 'Behavioral Sociology of Law: A Defense' (1986) 49 The Modern Law Review 262.
Cooter R, 'Law and Unified Social Theory' (1995) 22(1) Journal of Law and Society 50.
de Jong MJ, *Grootmeesters van de sociologie (Grant Masters of Sociology)* (Boom 1997).
Ellickson RC, 'Bringing Culture and Human Frailty to Rational Actors. A Critique of Classical Law and Economics' (1989) 65 (23) Chicago Kent Law Review 23.

Emmelman DS, 'The Effect of Social Class on the Adjudication of Criminal Cases: Class-Linked Behavior Tendencies, Common Sense, and the Interpretive Procedures of Court-appointed Defense Attorneys' (1994) 17(1) Symbolic Interaction 1.

Faure MG, *The Impact of Behavioral Law and Economics on Accident Law* (Boom Juridische Uitgevers 2009).

Frankford DM, 'Social Structure of Right and Wrong: Normativity without Agents' (1995) 20(3) Law & Social Inquiry 787.

Frey BS, *Not Just for the Money: An Economic Theory of Personal Motivation* (Edward Elgar 1997).

Hammersley M, 'Provoking Misunderstanding: A Comment on Black's Defence of Value-Free Sociology' (2014) 65(3) The British Journal of Sociology 492.

Harcourt BE, 'After the 'Social Meaning Turn': Implications for Research Design and Methods of Proof in Contemporary Criminal Law Policy Analysis' (2000) 34(1) Law & Society Review 179.

Hawkins K, *The Uses of Discretion* (Second Edition, Clarendon Press 2001).

Hembroff LA, 'The Seriousness of Acts and Social Contexts: A Test of Black's Theory of the Behaviour of Law' (1987) 93(2) American Journal of Sociology 322.

Horwitz AV, 'Resistance to Innovation in the Sociology of Law: A Response to Greenberg' (1983) 17 Law & Society Review 369.

Hunt A, 'Behavioral Sociology of Law. A Critique of Donald Black' (1983) 10(1) Journal of Law and Society 19.

Jolls C, Sunstein CR and Thaler R, 'Theories and Tropes. A Reply to Posner and Kelman' (1998) 50(5) Stanford Law Review 1593.

Kelman M, 'Behavioral Economics as Part of a Rhetorical Duet: A Response to Jolls, Sunstein, and Thaler' (1998) 50 Stanford Law Review 1577.

Korobkin RB and Ulen TS, 'Law and Behavioral Science: Removing the Rationality Assumption from Law and Economics' (2000) 88(4) California Law Review 1051.

Kuo S and others, 'Crime Reporting Behavior and Black's *Behavior of Law*' (2011) 27(1) International Sociology 51.

Lindenbergh SD and Mascini P, 'Schurende dilemma's in het aansprakelijkheidsrecht: De spanning tussen financiële en relationele compensatie' in Boom, W. H. van, I. Giesen and A. J. Verheij (eds), *Capita civilologie: Handboek empirie en privaatrecht* (Civilology Series, Boom Juridische uitgevers 2013).

Marshall DA, 'The Dangers of Purity: On the Incompatibility of 'Pure Sociology' and Science' (2008) 49 The Sociological Quarterly 209.

Mascini P, Mascini, Peter 'Risky Information: Social Limits to Risk Management' (1998) 6(1) Journal of Contingencies and Crisis Management 35.

–'Comparing Assumptions Underlying Regulatory Inspection Strategies: Implications for Oversight Policy' in Van Slyke, Shanna, Francis Cullen and Michael Benson (eds), *Oxford Handbook on White-Collar Crime* (2016).

Mitchell G, 'Why Law and Economics' Perfect Rationality Should Not Be Traded for Behavioral Law and Economics' Equal Incompetence' (2002) 91 The Georgetown Law Journal 67.

Posner RA, 'Rational Choice, Behavioral Economics, and the Law' (1998) 50(5) Stanford Law Review 1551.

Robbennolt JK, 'Behavioral Ethics Meets Legal Ethics' (2015) 11 Annual Review of Law and Social Science 75.

Rostain T, 'Educating Homo Economicus: Cautionary Notes on the New Behavioral Law and Economics Movement' (2000) 34(4) Law & Society Review 973.

Ryan P, 'Positivism: Paradigm or Culture?' (2015) 36(4) Policy Studies 417.

Senechal de la Roche R, 'Why is Collective Violence Collective?' (2001) 19(2 July) Sociological Theory 126.

Schroeder J, 'Just So Stories: Posnerian Methodology' (2001) 22 Cardozo Law Review 351.

Sunstein CR, 'Behavioral Law and Economics. A Progress Report' (1999) 6(1/2) American Law and Economics Review 115.

Schwitters RJS, *Recht en samenleving in verandering: Een inleiding in de rechtssociologie (Law and Society in Transformation: An Introduction in the Sociology of Law)* (Kluwer: Deventer 2008).

Tenbrunsel AE and Messick DM, 'Sanctioning Systems, Decision Frames, and Cooperation' (1999) 44 Administrative Science Quarterly 684.

Weber M, *Wirschaft und Gesellschaft* (J.C.B. Mohr 1925).

Weenink D, 'Een neurosociologisch perspectief op emoties Besprekingsartikel van David Franks en Thomas Smith Mind, brain and society: toward a neurosociology of emotion. (A Neurosociological Perpective on Emotions. Review Article of David Franks and Thomas Smith Mind, Brain, and Society: Towards a Neurosociology of Emotion.' (2009) 5(2) Sociologie 244.